True Faith

True Faith

POEMS BY

Ira Sadoff

AMERICAN POETS CONTINUUM SERIES, NO. 132

BOA EDITIONS, LTD. ⌁ ROCHESTER, NY ⌁ 2012

First Edition
12 13 14 15   7 6 5 4 3 2 1

For information about permission to reuse any material from this book please
contact The Permissions Company at www.permissionscompany.com or e-mail
permdude@eclipse.net.

Publications by BOA Editions, Ltd.—a not-for-profit corpo-
ration under section 501 (c) (3) of the United States Internal
Revenue Code—are made possible with funds from a variety
of sources, including public funds from the New York State
Council on the Arts, a state agency; the Literature Program of
the National Endowment for the Arts; the County of Monroe,
NY; the Lannan Foundation for support of the Lannan Trans-
lations Selection Series; the Mary S. Mulligan Charitable
Trust; the Rochester Area Community Foundation; the Arts
& Cultural Council for Greater Rochester; the Steeple-Jack
Fund; the Ames-Amzalak Memorial Trust in memory of Henry Ames, Semon
Amzalak and Dan Amzalak; and contributions from many individuals na-
tionwide. See Colophon on page 84 for special individual acknowledgments.

ART WORKS.
arts.gov

State of the Arts

NYSCA

Cover Design: Sandy Knight
Interior Design and Composition: Richard Foerster
Manufacturing: Thomson-Shore
BOA Logo: Mirko

Library of Congress Cataloging-in-Publication Data

Sadoff, Ira.
  True faith / by Ira Sadoff. — 1st ed.
      p. cm. — (American Poets Continuum Series; no. 132)
  ISBN 978-1-934414-82-8 (pbk. : alk. paper)
  I. Title.
PS3569.A26.T78 2012
811'.54—dc23
                        2011037245

BOA Editions, Ltd.
250 North Goodman Street, Suite 306
Rochester, NY 14607
www.boaeditions.org
A. Poulin, Jr., Founder (1938–1996)

The happy man only feels at ease because the unhappy bear their burdens in silence, and without that silence happiness would be impossible.

—Anton Chekhov, "Gooseberries"

Contents

I

II
Maybe

True Faith

True faith belongs to the truly unstable,
To those enormous sunflowers that keep crows away
With their bowed heads almost touching the garden floor.
The prayers of my friends too are passive-aggressive.
They begin with "I bet you're not listening, you bastard."

Then they incant some hard-bitten phrases
Learned by heart after they learned to be scathing
And doubt-ridden, after they heard "bed-ridden,"
After the coughing fits, the scams and the accidents
That sought them out. After weeks without sleep,

After some poor slave from Beijing steals their job
And a box store expects us to be grateful
For the toaster that costs fifty cents less
Even though it falls apart in our hands in an instant
The way we fall apart in an instant. We hate the factories

Anyway: the silver filings, the heating coils, the view
Of the brick building next to ours without windows.
It's ok, I spent my best years in a hamper, hiding
From my mother and father. You could see
Through the wicker there, and here I write a sentence

About banishment, the packed suitcase, the secret staircase.
I bring the others inside with me, we hold our breath.
It's one breath, it's the same breath. It's the hush
That chaperones someone as he flies off
The mountain top with just his nylon and aluminum wings

(It's not human), catching the thermal, circling
And descending, until he lands tumbleweed style
In a field adjacent to the vineyard of the Lord,
Followed by beers at the Hofbrau, where we lean
Into one another with joy and shout and toast one another,

Thinking we could have lost this one and that one,
And how quiet the earth would be, and how round.

In Madrid

When the Lord god went belly-up, out of business,
little brats went shin-kicking through the streets of Pamplona.
The watchmaker closed up shop to peel wallpaper off the Vatican.
Nietzsche was in my dream too, in a tedious spat
with Alma Mahler: the syphilis was invisible, so he thought
These are my *thoughts*. Sunny, a hundred degrees. Frozen daiquiris.
I wasn't going to let any sordid affair spill my happiness.
Until the Romanian chipped away at the *Pietà*.
He was driven, bipolar, mood disordered:
at least they could name him this. As for the dark stuff,
blank page after blank page, motives sail by
like an afternoon cloudburst, and I don't want to belabor
the matador, how speared he was, or how she came to me
in a black dress out of Manet and took me in her mouth,
and I'm whispering Dear god, what happened
to my reverence for clarity and a few simple rules of behavior?
Don't make me feel we're all drives and cracked hardware
wired wrong: I want to blame someone, I want to
paint over the underground where I'm waiting at 3 A.M.
for the train, and yes, I'm sure I'm being followed.

American

First time and only time I met LeRoi
we were standing at the Five Spot bar—summer '61:
he was drunk, disgracefully so, which is why

he deigned to talk to me in my white oxford shirt
and hair fluffed up for a future
ivy-league career: I hadn't yet read *The Toilet*

or *The Slave*, I'd only been fucked twice
by two girls from Queens
with hairdos like spider-legs. I hadn't yet

thrown a brick through IBM's window,
been gassed at Rockefeller Center—maybe once
I'd climbed stairs to the War Resisters League,

picked up an A.J. Muste pamphlet or two.
I might have lived on meringue pies
at the Automat, worked the register at Gristedes.

I remember most of what happened, since
I was sixteen, self-assured, sensitive in the worst way—
no one had even laid a hand on me

yet—but then he raised his black turtleneck
to show me the swollen welts on his ribs
where a cop had throttled him and I had the gall

to insist, "I'm not like that: I'm no racist."
"You just want me to like you," he shrugged,
then the second set began. The next man I met

that tanked up on rage was Archie Shepp.
Every riot you could think of had burned
a putrid city down. For my thirtieth birthday,

he played two short cuts, breathy midrange
off-pitch squawks, shouted the drummer offstage,
then gave us that stare since there was no one

else to look at, to look at what we'd become.

Lament

While I was gone I lost my finches.
The first lilies bloomed. The second and third.
My town lost a lamp store and light in its windows.
My camellias, how pale they seem.
And the grass, how impatient, acting out
With its spray of weeds. Hummingbirds,
I am so sorry. I fell in love a little while I was gone.
I sugared a few doughnuts in her kitchen.
I liked it best when we fumbled around
In the pitch searching for each other.
In the silences there was a great sea between us.
All right, it was more like a pond. But an icy little pond.
My finches, how they would dip and peck.
How bright they were. The finches: how I miss them.

Down by the Old Mill Stream

                        For instance,
the shallow river was bronze, fish were breathing
along the bank, swelling and deflating, but I don't remember
the green things—if they were natural/unnatural.
                                In the right light
you could see through them, the scaly creatures
we came from, the way
you could almost see through the statue of David.
You could almost taste the phosphorescence of the ocean
in that one dented half-rusted tin cup no one gave me.

I would only lie down with one person, and she
had not yet arrived, because that was before
the plane was shaking, before bombs fell, before the apple,
well, jesus, it took a while to figure out the flaws
in that story. Let there be no more *in a former life*
or *I've always been under the impression.*
Let the mothers keep their children in the shelter
a few hours more. Because there's nothing like water
slipping through your fingers to teach you a lesson.

The Sound and the Fury (1991)

My friends, the catastrophes came to greet me.
Of pleasure, I'd had too much. Erasure
was the order of the day. Goodbye lover, goodbye
house and home, goodbye life's savings.

One is increasingly minor, which is one way
to fly low over the city
where Tyson bit off Evander's ear,
then Van Gogh's ear, the ear of my ex-wife.

But I too was hounded by a piercing cry.
Maybe it was just a crow; more likely
one of those turgid voices inside struck me
with that dizzying just-hit-your-head feeling,

as if god's emissary had entered me
in a dream or on some lower rung on the ladder,
a brocade of shadow and light so clearly chiseled out
that, ok, my speech was three feet ahead of me.

Oyster Bay

The stench came from the other side of the beach,
or so we thought, since we couldn't see their faces.

That they were probably Black, that they didn't want
the inside of our wallets, that we hid their music

in the closets, is so much pentimento
for the scoliosis. Ditto what we did in bed,

what thousands do with sharp instruments,
or what I wore in Calcutta when I saw

through poverty as the shaggy dress it is:
no romance to it, that singing from the alley.

Its thick vibrato, no Maria Callas in it, no high C beauty.
I want to end this with a view of the bay, the hush

and shhhh of design: my father scribbling plans
on driftwood, instilling goodness in us,

the kind of goodness that spreads shmaltz
on a butter knife then wipes it on his pants: what a god

he was, inscrutable and terrible in unequal doses.

Apologia

I was raised on impudence and finger-pointing,
a handful of addenda and nevertheless-buts.
I want to argue your god with you, god of miracles,

the god who repaired the arthritic arm without surgery,
who sculpted those beautiful oiled-up beauties
at the beach who listen to music made of two notes, maybe

three, whose conversation could be stored inside the skull
of a finch. So whose fault is it I can't bear
their happiness? Why was I in awe when the Romanian

took a chisel to the *Pietà*, and even if that's technically
not true, where's the joy in horseradish
that makes our eyes tear up? Why not throw a tantrum

as they break glass at the wedding party? I may be low
on mendacity but a few items distress me dearly:
how much time's lost on staggering betrayals, many

perpetuated by yours truly. I don't know who's inside
my body strutting and squirming, twice the size of California,
making the fir trees barely visible, the human race a thimble,

but something sordid makes my lips purse, something pure
exhaust smoke. I step aside from those
who've been anointed to hear voices: they're like bees

under your pant leg that sting and sting, so even
when they're dead because they hurt you, the flesh
is still gristle, swelling and pulsing: that's where my god is.

On Style

In conversation I have but one gear
on my bicycle: always climbing the hill, laboring,
questing, asking questions like *What hurt you*

when you were young? or *How can you believe*
in god after that? My style sends people
up the wall: they make up stories about me,

they psychoanalyze my deficiencies.
That's ok: we all want to know each other better.
There's something niggling about me too—

I can rave about the Vatican (what a tourist trap!),
but once inside the chapel a stranger
collapses, there's a doctor leaning over her in prayer

with a pocketknife he opens up her trachea
and the gasp of air that's her life
hushes everyone, lets me know I've been

wrong, but let's change the subject:
are there hills where you live
and can you ride your bike there?

My Country

Decipher me, we say to the wilderness.
Perhaps we need our own private radios.
If so, I'd be a station with too much static.

Moreover, that sense-making trick
where you follow a thread
from beginning to end, is wearing thin.

Perhaps you'd like a little history
to accompany the bloody nonsense.
Like Lorca's toast to Franco, the bodega

on a side street where his murmurs
mean less than mudslides in the public arena.
There they'd shoot you for thinking,

whereas here they soften you up
while you ripen until it's a little muddy
in the brain field. Foggy too—to enjoy

the indoor shopping. They give you maps
to locate your heart's desires,
but when it's over there's a heat wave

inside your head: there, the bulls of Pamplona.

2.

You could say I was delusional, stressed out
when I rode the pampas with Lorca,
you could say imagination got the better of me.

But I'm a sensible person, not prone to delirium,
not the kind who stampedes past the crowd
to simper before the eviscerated flesh of movie stars.

My dad was a starry-eyed sad sack who ran away
with a lounge singer from Budapest. In her sequined dress
she outshone casino lights on the edge of Vegas.

He bet everything on her. Everything meaning nothing,
meaning I'm getting out of this country:
you can have it, Perry Como and Rosemary Clooney,

you can have Bob Sadoff and whatever you do for him.
He's nothing to me, nothing like Lorca, who
I keep in my little boy's knapsack with apples and pears,

a bridle and serenades by Rodrigo and Tárrega.
They take me to prairies where *stipa*
can flourish, but rarely a tree, and surely Lorca

saw this meadow as a place to camp and sing,
since clouds were stirring and future beefsteaks
of America blocked the road to the next bodega.

The dew-soaked grasses seem like his slicked-down hair
I hear him combing: it sounds like a small boat
scissoring the water, followed by a few shots in the alley.

I swear there's a worm in the brain of every boy
who crosses the border, barefoot and dreamy.
From the foothills of the Sierras he can see Granada.

A few silver coins and the moon in his pocket.

Blue Catamarans

Where *they* grew up, blue catamarans
snugged the harbor. The back-then Blacks and Italians
roped them to anchor. Then they knifed each other late at night

and I don't blame them. The moon over Oyster Bay
should remain with erased populace, just as you'd scrub your hair
for lice. After work, I beat flounder with a baseball bat.

My friends weren't books, after all.
We were made sassy by holes in an undershirt.
Before the skin was kindling, long before

you took your shirt off to the spume and spray
of the ocean, leaning into all that infinite,
where did that get you? How did you like to be

spoken to? Might you like to be passed by,
to be thought of as a meaningless venomous person.
To be reviled, mind-numbing, tedious, dull?

I'm vaguely familiar with exits and squad cars,
have laminated my personal dramas in many documents.
But my interest here is in the beach and the catamaran.

Many catamarans come from tropical islands
where television's a bad, sexy nightmare. If only I'd known,
when I picked up a shell, this nasty smelling shell, on the beach

after a gull dropped it from a very high place.

Surely the Wind

Surely the wind would speak of violence
if the wind would speak. But also valence

when you think of airplanes and their weight
buoyed up and floating, seemingly still

and noiseless—which is how things look
far off, dimly lit: a father's lips blazing

as he dies, slipping in and out of sentences,
sentences that mean so much I can't keep them

by the hospital bed. Better in his kitchenette.
Back there, his voice was hoarse

from shouting. It wasn't a plea, it wasn't flat
and horizon-filled, like the plains.

It wasn't plain speaking either. It was an animal
bray, chomping at the bit when you broke him.

Water Musik

The gods keep depicting us in our weedy randomness.
They buzz and strafe as if *we* dirtied the water.

We stride away from them, away from the river.
The still river, muddy, debris-skimmed:

seldom is a barge on the Thames a musical occasion.
But seldom is sawdust the story of the tree.

And just because a knife is not a finch wing,
just because we sing jagged arias underwater,

because the standard catalogue of shadows pass over,
it doesn't mean Blouse, Coffin, Notes on a Napkin.

A California quail flusters out of the bushes.
The box of candy opens, Mother, do you remember?

Worry Fills the Brim of My Hat

Mother could temper the willow,
the willow by the river
where she strayed, saying nonsense

to a tree, a tree she found listing.
What little she saw was her savior.
But the words were hieroglyphics,

the jumble of syllables we utter
when we approach the unsayable.
How calm the willow stayed

as the river came up to meet it.
What a well the self would be
if we could find it. I worry

about her in her nightgown,
she who's long gone.
I worry how our minds fill

and empty. As for the tongue,
you can almost feel it
swelling out of its casing,

limber and directionless.

All the Secrets Are Not Scars

Padlocked, the old family mansion.
Enthrall, master and depict,
all ether, unavailable. Over this predicament,
the skull is a mountain.

Other tortured resemblances include
the cliff's my precipice.
Somewhere else she's spitting into a cup.
Dandelion and ragweed stand in

for a family's fortune. The tale in transit,
between being lathered up
and being artistically brushed by one last
self-portrait. The body apologizes

for its flaws. All the secrets are not scars.
All the regress does not address.
Still we feel
for a pulse, the métier to pursue.

Let us thrum through neighboring woods
then, the counseling woods.
To keep the bees away we forgo the swelling,
the visible pinprick on the forearm,

the fever-pitch aftermath.

Adam

So little time left to ruin: I hardly have a minute
to cover up those old rapid-fire faux pas
that left my head turned around, staring into the wreckage,
the old void in my mother, the extraction the minute I was born.

Some rituals die slowly, so the stupid parts of us stay shamed.
When we make ourselves small and sinister,
what nakedness is worth watching? As for our bosses, god,
the Father, the registrar, former lovers and commanders,

our insufficiencies excite them, so they lock doors to their
        offices
and do what they do there. I am not concerned with being
        unloved.
Not concerned about a parking space, the mistake
in my checkbook, sour milk in the Frigidaire, not the state

of my soul after a series of drinking binges.
So what is it that incites me, that shadows me with a rucksack,
with a deep raspy voice? A few childhood songs just before bed,
oh and those lanterns—it's New Year's in Beijing—the slate's

graced with calligraphy, all the elaborate figures
and signs— I don't know a thing about them. They're assigned
their own gods and devils, they can't see me close up,
they have their own basilicas, they minister

to their loyal citizens their own shrieks and yammers.

In Virginia

In Virginia they have their drawl and their dogwood,
they've got tactile humidity and a history
that's slavish. They love ideas in Virginia. Virginia's a person
who loves to stall at the malls. She doesn't like
to pay shipping. She doesn't like to drive around town
to save few cents on gas. Am I being too specific? Is there no
Virginia in you? The dancing torso that knows nothing
about tiny sensors they implant to make you want things?
There's a hole in the self: you can't throw a penny down deep
    enough.
They still have dirt floors in Virginia. Real other-side-
of-the-tracks folks who shine your sweat and mop.
In Virginia we bash mailboxes with baseball bats,
we shake our catalpa pods and we don't talk to stranglers
in that shanty town where we grew up separately.
Virginia, you are my girlfriend, lover, partner, wife,
the one I come back to late at night,
whose fluttery eyelids ship her off to some sleepy island
where a mountain ridge insanely hovers.

In a Southern Climate

All the ambience of Texas once brought me to my knees.
I wanted to praise their wide-brim hats and long cascading lines
to churches, but not the sudden dust storms and downpours

that dim the city of Houston to the charred shade of gray
of concrete yards where prisoners at Guantánamo
still stroll to dreamy tunes by Iron Butterfly an hour a day.

You cannot make up Texas, you who only knew
the President and the President's cabinet, the President's Yes men
and Yes women, the swagger, the high-mindedness.

There was nothing candid there, nothing of nature's shine
reflected on the river (where we don't belong
except to muddy the surface), where black-crowned herons

settle on one foot in the Rio Grande, their minds occupied
by nothing but fish, one particular silver catfish—
they couldn't care less about the crappie, the bullhead, a school

of pickerel—when I'm inside the head of a heron I think
we're so much alike, so much more and less alone.
Oh my seismograph, you are such a personal feeling. A minor
figure,

of little import raised to the nth power. But how could I stand
here
on one foot all day, pretending you can't see me?
Was I just a little shiver dipping my beak into the water?

Dies Irae

I suspect it's the Dies Irae that gets me going, shaking a fist
at the gathering storm clouds I use as a symbol
of *The sky's a rotten apricot in my pocket.*

Just because the gods made us weave through traffic,
my fellow countrymen think it's fine to turn the oak
into a parking lot, to turn a hillside to a dog on a leash.

The requisite trumpets take me to the War now,
though really, delight in music
is unspeakable, the way it drills little spells inside you:

the Vienna woods are there, a shabby apartment in Prague
with a wooden slab for a bed and a giant cockroach
to sing to. So why do I need words too, a garbled shoebox

of sentences to poke through, a few figurines
that sit on the side of the bed
injecting me with their panic attacks? There they are,

cutting themselves in the mirror, singing
an aria from *Don Carlos*, and if you don't know
what they do to each other, look it up, look into their faces.

II

Maybe

If the sun and moon should doubt
They'd immediately go out.
                    —William Blake

Orphans

I cannot fawn
Dear Lord—oh I see
You tinker

With temperatures,
Bringing loves
For some to bury.

My friends
The diasporas
Shake a few fists

At your favored clouds
About to storm.
I won't deny

Parishioners' joys—
With faces both
Coming and going.

I too want a bliss
Like theirs:
Blankened or beautied.

Question

How did Yahweh
Become a still
Small voice and not
A thunderclap?

In moments
Of transition, the gods
Depart: to translate
Into scripture,

There is none like you
Among The gods,
O Lord, so the Agape
Must search out

The vacated houses,
Although the word
Agapeh once implied
A genuine affection

And deep love
Of the goddess,
Of goodness
We misheard.

Objectively, in Church

The house
Is rocking: blues
Waves a hand
Above the head
And the fingers
Wiggle like
Signifiers. I like
Singing to no one
Just like this.

A Mighty Fortress

A mighty fortress
I'm not, Dear god.
I'm just a flimsy
Little number, hanging
From Bond Street
In 1908; I can't
Afford to live
In a kingdom
I'd call a tenement.
I can't behold
The works
Of desolation
Wrought by no one
In particular
But daily
Abrade my sisters
Who take
In laundry. So
Individual they are,
You might miss them
In the next
Lightning storm.

Diagnosis

What did you think
Of yourself? Stricken,
A Once Favored Nation,
A former savior,
A little Satchmo,
Decrepit and diseased
But still breathing
Hard? 1971: "What
A Wonderful World":
Mount Etna
Erupts, Attica erupts,
The end of the War
Bubbles up, end
Of Empire's on edge,
The country dodders
Over its millionaires.
Light my cigarette
With your sawbucks,
Big Daddy, then
Warm yourself
A little number
By the Hot Five
Over an oil drum
With two-by-fours.

The War

Is a holy war.
Wholly
Scratch your ass
Then get in
The death box:

Say your prayers
Senators:
In the next
Wife you'll harbor
Resentments—

Out of habit
The kill word
Will cross your lips,
A memorandum

Pointed at a person.

Chamber Pot

In the vestibule,
You are obsolete
As we are, we
Scribblers, poets
And painters, pianists
And toe-pointers,
We Solomons
Who worry for
Sons and daughters,
How no one will sing
For them the way
Whitman once chirped
His lament in public.
In his arms,
Soldiers and lovers,
Those who lived
In secret in the country
Of our birth.

Once I Could Say

Once I could say
Loyal friend,
The house wren.

I might even sing
To him. Didn't I
hear the beatific,

The breathlessness
In the patter of voice
Shaking the tamarind,

The feathery bright
Green foliage
Stammered by a breeze?

Those muttering
Implosions, did nothing
Intend them? When

The wren took his awl
To the infested branch
He fed an idea there.

Like Magic

Just as I decide
There's nothing true
About me (can't tell

If I'm more despised
Or ignored, my mind's
Warding off or reeling in

Someone who could scald me
With a spoon of chatter),
Just then I decide

In my seclusion there's a cabin
By the stream and the jangled speech
Of a person is hushed enough

So I say *Hello No One,*
Can you hear me?
In the rushes I spook

A few geese into flight.

Stirhouse

I was shopping around
In the storehouse
Of lovers, looking for
Not an icon
Exactly, no one
To kneel down to
Praise, no one
To do my dirty work—
The work of
Stripping down to
Take a look, a good look
At what we call
Aftermath—having loved,
Having been scarred
And seared fingers
Used for touch,
I'm not looking
For one fresh
Out of the box.

The Gift

I think of this pendant as an estuary
and I think of the estuary
as a god everyone drifts or swims to,
because what choice do they have
in the delta but to drown
New Orleans again or submit
to "higher powers"? What
would you do, given
such a gift? Mine's
a Sterling Silver Marcasite
& Garnet Glass Heart Pendant:
~~$70.00~~ but only $50.00 on Amazon.com.
I am still a boy who as a boy
swam in that estuary. Every river came to me
just for the asking. I never found a pendant there,
some charm that might speak to me
and the rivers, and if the rivers were friends
you could see why I could go there.

Elegy

I tried to stay in the open moment,
the instant perfectly empty:
there's a casket there,
resting, pure silk and mahogany.
The lining may have been lead
and in the rowboat I remember
my regret, having left the island
with all my imperfections
paying attention to the gesture
but not the person no longer a person.
In good times there were ledges
and seals, the cormorants came back,
and the rusty shipwreck was a site
of devotion for those of us
who'd like to preserve a moment
or drag it with us, the living.

III

Unhappy that I am, I cannot heave my heart into my mouth.
—Cordelia, *King Lear*

For night owls shriek where mounting larks should sing
—King Richard, *King Richard the Second*

America II

At last we were struck with a great sorrow, a dark passage
in a Gothic Cathedral, a little strip of light
from the window shining down on the marble floor,
the light cut into strips mixed in with debris

from workers' shoes. They were already
filling in the frescos with pauses, clouds of plaster
on pallets of wood. They restored the surfaces
the way makeup restores faces, except that close-up

we're layered with happenstance and very few
end up pink and refreshed. You can see
erosion in our expressions, as in a Bacon painting
where a face seems twisted by a scream

while the rest of the body minds its business.
Some strayed into strangers' apartments,
then or later, some saw their jobs as circling
a block, as losing patience, losing lovers,

losing jobs, biting their lips, thinning their hair.
A few had been hosed down by police
decades ago, and the force of that water reminds them
of resistance, those clubbing shots, the shoves

that pushed us to the ground or brought us
to our knees to pray. But much remains unknown
about our fevers, those hungers
that have no words around them, no illustrations.

The Aftermath

At first absence did not rush in.
Its brevity was a pause,
a cancellation, a sudden clearing

past the moss beds under the pines.
No more strolls through the old woods,
the same muddy tracks, same old stream.

Of course it was a lull, a blackout:
forgetting makes sleep the salve it is.
I woke to that inky, bottomless hush

that stamps afternoons when you've missed
a morning or can't wait for night to end.
Other mourners want a story stitched up

and ready, they want the next song to play,
they want to shop and love each other.
They want the untrained eye

to forgive the disappearing snow
where that patch of grasslessness
welcomes back the wrens and juncos.

Who can bear those voices, all that singing?

Lapses

I can't just be tracking the lapses,
the deprived and lovelorn about to leap from the ledge,
leaving out the feathery transient random

melodies, some centuries old,
whole symphonies that still stir that stew of fantasy
and biology somewhere inside the calliope

we call the senses. And what is it about
being naked, for example, that made Whitman crazy,
made him a peacock display of self-pleasure?

And why can I still see him ghostly on the ferry
rubbing against strangers who think his touch accidental?
You can almost hear Methodist hymnals inside them

as they look for a property beside the grave site
they're entitled to, to save them from this mindful business,
when all those other tenses—those jobs and promises

and bruises flake away like rust on a barge
before it's repainted that toenail shade of red. So
we must go out to sea, the boundless, bountiful sea

of old literatures, with which we imbue
water imagery—I say *imbue* because I write for myself
and strangers. I try to shape my strangeness

with speed and gravity, the confusion
you uncover just getting to unknow yourself, the part
that's celibate and monklike, without the flies around it.

Before

This was before the current reign of terror.
Before Gentlemen start your engines.
Before they reported *salient to your habitat*.

Even in our small town, one of those
single-street hamlets shoved against a ridge,
the hills were all snow and sunlight:

echoes and shadows were missing.
I think there were a few loons on the lake,
one hummingbird lathering a camellia.

What stirred us then was strictly unfettered.
I suppose caveats were sad to be invented.
They brought on the chants of Russian monks

(—*oh gladsome radiance*—), those bass and baritones
who gave birth to earthquakes and creaking
dungeon doors with cavernous, rumbling voices.

Their illegible syllables became the gulags of tomorrow.
Maybe a few were dreaming privately.
But once they dug a few ditches and finger-pointing

became an outdoor sport, the devout were like bees
when the apiarist takes off his veil. And the stings:
you might think the fates had dispensed their arrows.

Id

It comes from that voice dogs can hear, the glass-
breaking high C that makes life sylphlike.
Of course sylphlike's

for pussies. If I say I want a dancer's body,
I don't want to dance: I want to be lithe,
lasting a little longer to take in

the traffic jams. I don't want to look inward,
reflect on, stare at my reflection, nail
another deer on the mantle. Be indelible—

all cobble and boarded-up windows.
Dear reader, I left cupboards open
for your perusal. So trespass my secrets:

I have never cast the petulance aside,
not even just sat with that humlessness.
Can I call that my own personal abyss?

I'm not exempt, I'm no special case, I won't
go around with scissors and a razor blade,
cutting into things, inspecting, shutting down

the operation. I don't want to say nimbus
when I mean shotgun. Or be my friend
when I mean slip it in. Penthouse,

when I mean pent-up house.

Self-Portrait

I sniff after the sparrow and the spaniel, flitting around,
barking, digging up the dirt: how could I not be
at one with them? But I'm a spendthrift too, rummaging about

old sport coats, selecting a style, a clash of styles—
in a private moment trying to decide who I am today by trying on
something discarded, something nobody treasured—

I think I want everyone and everything to be loved so much
I get dour, chastising, dark, and sometimes hate
so much I can't go for a stroll without recycling the moment

they dropped acid on my palm, the thousand ways I could ease
their demise—dipping them into a river of invective
that seems futile and enticing—whether it's the Secretary of
State

or a species of white shirts and thin black ties who exude
smugness,
who quote from the bible as if it were the Bible. It's like having
an affair—
they all end badly, don't they?—thereby the passion flies out of me

like an open window in February: take the heat, world,
disperse it before I undress another thought.

While in Brooklyn

Only one person broke a bottle over your head.

You could strut, you could knock someone
off their perch, pore over their wardrobe
with wise remarks, you could steal a few notions

from the grocer. You could treat a ball field
like a battlefield, you could scar a cheek,
steal the thunder of the little genius and snap

his pens in two. In a pinch you could deliver
for the dry cleaner. You could make sense
of a block, on a good day a half-mile square,

but after that if you cross the bridge
to the marsh that's a swamp you're lucky
if you see a young blue crab squirm

in a stranger's palm. Refineries tower over
the Arthur Kill. Satellites radiate
invisible messages from no one you would know.

There's a government here, a world order
with its cattails and oil spills,
and just under the surface a corpse or two.

For Beauty

For beauty I keep a ceramic swan
Aunt Millie gave me when I was three:
it makes me think of muffins and cornbread

and a sour jug of milk. Never am I happier
than licking pistachio gelato
at Perchè no!, strolling to the Duomo

and looking up at all those heavenly faces.
My reports from the planet earth
have been dismal, serpentine, prone to nicks and cuts.

I always miss the moment when time stretches out
and the human flesh is cloudlike
and fragrant. In one episode I'm so close

to the stage the cellist's every gesture sings
to me, her every eye-flutter
suggests the otherworldly; can I say even now

I hear violins in the background: they're steam clouds
that hover over those who can't balance their books,
whose love lives are strewn with impassible interludes?

But there's my father coming to tuck me in—
I'm dreaming now—to beg forgiveness
long after he's dead. My forehead's blessed.

Imagination's a great gift: you can make it small,
call it escapist, transcendent, fancy, and sometimes
it walks away from the accident; it might haul you off

to a lush little meadow, or the muddy pond
where yaks dip their tongues in the gatorless water
where you can wash off the scratches and bruises.

What I Meant

What I meant by sunshine—cheerful, willful, chipper—
are salvageable parts, but what about broken,
sullen people who can't bear

a shred of felicity? They work late into the night,
stack pants at Sam's Club, they teach
six-year-olds "Frère Jacques"

in Cherry Hills. They get bristly on line at Shaw's
since they're ants on mountains of sugar;
they come out from under shoes

and sandwich plates peddling their goods,
and by goods I mean tin cups we fill
with quarters for off-key hymns

they sing to the sidewalk. We try to straighten out
our soured love affairs, the mangled
sentences we've been given,

but when we address each other with our terrible
knowledge how deeply open life is—
I can't tell if it's a well

or a chasm, but at least it's not the frenzied little busy
who pretends to be sorry, the one who says,
Blank me, Jazz me up, Fill me in.

In My Little Paradise

So overgrown, the yellow poppies
keel over. After so much beauty,

after the heat spells of August,
a full house and then an empty house,

sweeping up to a little music
(a favorite cup dropped from a shelf),

too many attachments here:
who drank from which glass,

who couldn't bear a phrase,
who became so shrill I'd shrink back

from what's imprinted there. How to take
those ragged bursts of color now,

or the kerchief left behind, a scent
that lingers longer than the person.

How can I keep my own head up
when having been inside someone

is like breathing deeply, but also
having blood drawn?

Ex-Wives

In summer, impalas
feed on young shoots of grass;
in winter on herbs and shrubs where grasslands

meet the savannah, so we don't worry
for their breed. Even as individual
breathing animals, impalas stay invisible

to us, like asides. Graceful, territorial,
we still hear their voices
as they're vaguely piping. Their species

thrive on the plains, even when
they're slaughtered wholesale by jackals,
pythons and baboons. With their white bellies,

their chestnut coats, leaping forays,
we cannot hold onto them
skittering across the plains. Whatever suddenness

makes their hearts race, they are great joys
for all we pour into them
that is not them. We pour into them

the river that rises to their lapping tongues,
the heat that makes their chests expand
and contract like accordions: they play familiar tunes

on a street corner, but not on the street where you live.

My First Roses

My first roses brought me to my senses.
All my furies, I launched them like paper boats
in the algaed pond behind my house.

First they were pale, then peach and blood red.
You could be merciless trimming them back.
You could be merciless and I needed that.

Emerald green with crimson tips,
these were no crowns of thorns.
They would not portend nor intimate.

But if you fed them they'd branch out:
two generations in a single summer.
One had a scent of fruit & violet, the other

blazed up, a flotilla of lips on the lawn.

Country Living

I was just forgetting the stroll grandpa took with Grieg,
then I forgot the blessings
bestowed on me by Jesus, and the amber light at dusk

that made me think the world was somewhere else aflame,
because right now someone's roasting a pig on a spit,
and you can still hear its squeals in the shitpile

they call southern Ohio, where he was once mucking around,
happy as Stanley Plumly. You might not know
Stanley Plumly and you might not know Ronan O'Brien,

who plays the lyric suites as if he and Grieg had a score to settle
(each melody sparking his synapses with surgical precision),
and you might not know the caress of my former wife

when I was distressed, which took up a lot of clock time,
or how we'd visit soup kitchens and shelters
because we tried to think of ourselves as a good people,

and even though the stockbrokers of Brazil may think differently,
our lyric poets believe the body's made for pleasure,
and though you might not know Whitman's "Passage to India,"

or that all the riches of the east were meant for our pleasure,
just as the pig was meant for our pleasure,
and Cambodians and the Shiites, and all of god's music,

and on the porn sites you'd think every young woman's pussy
was designed for our pleasure: to hear them squeal
on a spit you'd think what songs we are, what instruments,

walking with our hands behind our backs as if they were tied,
strolling through Grieg's meadow, talking
about claret, the kroner and the first trillium in the lea.

Happenstance

Happenstance, my hero, my bad habits
I wear like a Sunday dress
at the church social. I am more and more

a fan of *chicanery*
and other obsolete words to indicate joy
that's done and gone.

Where are the cantatas, the canned pears
in wine sauce, where is the first
Ms. Sadoff, and where the second? My mother

will live forever in her bitter claim
on solitude, peering from behind the window.
The empty house isn't empty enough:

moments battered by stepping over them
become silver here, chips of paint
from the radiator shining as I make my way

through the dark spaces so I can save
on electricity, so I don't shape
my thoughts around what's missing,

throwing shawls around them
to give them life and warmth (so essential
in a cold spell). Here are the dances

of and by the fireplace, here are the repasts,
the chow times, here are the little digs
and the private asides where you assigned

your virtues and my vices. Here is
out my very window the yellow window
of November, window of each November,

as long as there are Novembers to remember.

To the Gods

In the pre-regret phase, when I was flammable,
inviolate, a fortress, you could say
I was too particular and when I say particular

I mean fussy, and by fussy I mean
the period of self-study was a bad piano lesson.
Maybe a sweetness came over me, the dreamy

madness of darkening next to someone.
I had the swagger of someone
who made plans for the woodlands.

Maybe I was just a terrible shithead
with the patina of a principled person,
but in those days I had no idea

what ciphers we could be, what souvenirs,
what sad little bunnies, and there
the story veers, since there's no myself here,

or there's a chorus of voices vying for attention.
If I could sing I'd want to distill the thrill
of her, and more I'd want that lilting playful voice

to stay with me, all the sing-song iambs
that forestall the crash of loving
too much, hanging on too long. How can I

embrace the spell-makers and their hovering
cherubim, their harps and gladioli,
the gods who should have looked after me?

The Numbness

The numbness was wearing off,
& my tongue, thick as it was, vaguely recalled
its vital functions: to lick humidity
the body produces when over-heated. Most days
it's used on superiors. While a lucky few
weekend by the waterfront & drink each other in,
spurred on by whatever closed curtains indicate,
I am scampering along in this manner,
taking the stairs two at a time
to my own personal hell—you know,
after you've fallen, some bastard's pushed you
from behind, have you ever tried screaming then?
I was feeling deeply, how small the mouth is.
How small and open. How blank
the hours after work, how cavernous comes next—
then someone's calling from the human race,
there's a rescue party, someone tugs on the rope
and a child appears from the bottom of the mine shaft.

Because We Have Failed So Often

and we betray as we've been betrayed, because in our heads
we're high priests while in our pants we operate
on a cash basis, we can't afford to judge. We can't exclude

our neighbors, old lovers, complete strangers. Except
that President who was a murderer and a liar,
and pedophiles and drunks, drunks who were bullies,

smug characters too, advice-givers. There's certain music—
country or jazz—that sets us on edge, and we abhor
craters left by a drone that smashed the home

of some great-aunt of a Taliban. So it's hard to say
what's left besides bodies in a ditch,
our hard-heartedness, brittle as shell, because we've failed

so often, betrayed and been betrayed, because we're lost
without each other and there are two melodies
in our heads, one for each ear, one by Wagner with anvils

and horns, the other by Mozart, with strings and bassoons.

At the Polynesian Paradise in the Mall of America

When the plaster casters placed Jimi Hendrix's enormous cock
    on display
in the museum of Great Ideas, I knew the Era
of white suits and mint juleps, the Era of the New Criticism,
    the Era
of thinking about Eras, was gone. Someone took a ball-peen
    hammer

to the clean underwear drawer. The coarseness of the concept
    of brassieres
was laid on a junk heap outside the New York Public Library steps.
I guess unhinged isn't too strong a word to describe
the brouhahas, the upstarts hissing at those who carried the
    Talmud

on the A train, or those who believed in the drip-down theory
of Economics since their uncles once broke bread with Milton
    Friedman.
Look it up, I want to say. This is no bite down on a mushroom
hallucination complete with sitar music. This is history

with doors tacking off their frames, with a hinge or two missing.

In the course of Human Events, I have no fucking idea.
Not a glimmer, not even a grimace can appear on my face
without faking the act of faith like some overworked cop
who rattles off the virtues of writing out tickets

and kicks half-dressed indigents off sewer grates in winter
so young couples from Orlando can view the displays

of Christmas scenes from Hans Christian Anderson as a puppet
     show.
My friends, my vicissitudes, there's something Sufi about me

this afternoon as I wander through the mall
in my tennis shoes, looking for nothing, nothing in particular.
Sometimes the whole world smells like salmon to me.
Sometimes salmon blackened with tarragon and mango sauce,

which I find a comforting reminder of the tropics,
completely manufactured, of course, for the Early Bird Specials,
which brings me back to the Era of preconceived ideas
about goodness and terror, about kindness and terror, about
     terror

and more terror. Even in college I never tasted
red wine this putrid, even in college I never listened
to the booth next door as a confessional,
where they must choose between the spaghetti platter

and their beta-blockers, where they weigh the virtues
of a panic-stricken night against that cheesecake they love
like life itself. Maybe that's why they shout at each other,
these relics of civilization: to make themselves heard.

Dispel Me

Dispel me, Jesus, if you're not too business.
I'm sliding down the slothful passages
to that heavy-lidded place

where I'm money, office, disingenuous.
Helping hand, excess sweetness.
I look out into blank and peaceful:

quiet, indirection, the most vaporous
of solutions. I look out into blank
and peaceful as if the whole purpose

of the storm were to overturn the skiff.
To shear off... But drowning's
adjacent to breathless, being there

as Violetta sings the last startling aria.
Inflicting and sewing up wounds
when what we require is air and music.

Revival

I was standing between two screams:
shortcomings the virus I spread through a crowd.
This time the stage was heated and galloping,
and vital life forces were the sheen of a horse's back
after a run. The water was choppy too
when the nun removed her habit
and waded into the river. Wading into the river
was an act of faith, not a mandate.
This woman, lover of Christ, as I'm
the lover of Christ, wants him to raise us up
past storm warnings and electrical pulses,
past detonating impulses, wants us
to rise above the given flesh. On my knees,
coughing before the mother of Pearl, I'm shoeless
at the shore of the river, dipping my foot in.

Heavens

Ok, it's sunny, otherworldly, skin-tight
where we're flabby and clouded over, pining away
under layers of jealousy, detachment, the compost heap

of the shucked and dismissed. Out of the bad deeds,
screeches in the arboretum, the wronged person
who circles the rotaries, the infidel

who torments her clitoris, the young man
who discovers he's nameless,
muttering when he should be moaning, shattering

the window of opportunity because—I forget where
I was going with this—perhaps the baffling
cataclysmic lesions that scar us invisibly—

but I suspect, deep down, we're a good people,
easily humbled: we implore, fill with worry,
we try to sing to loved ones, shadow

their wishes, color their hair as they fly
into the great nothing: no more, that's it.
But we can only hold the shell of them,

get on our knees and scrub away
the whole heavy saga. In another world,
people would know exactly how bad we are,

how we seize a dance floor, how we shake
and sweat profusely, how we hum a few bars
through the dead spots, and since we have no idea

what comes next, we set the homestead
ablaze. We bargain, we finagle,
we comb the hair on the corpses, their beautiful hair.

Acknowledgments

Many of these poems appeared (often in earlier versions and occasionally with different titles) in the following magazines:

American Poet: "My Country";

The Alaska Review: "Id";

The American Poetry Review: "Adam," "All the Secrets Are Not Scars" (originally as "Padlocked"), "A Mighty Fortress," "At the Polynesian Paradise in the Mall of America," "Blue Catamarans," "Chamber Pot," "Diagnosis," "Dies Irae," "Dispel Me," "Happenstance," "Heavens," "Id," "In Madrid," "Lapses," "Like Magic," "Objectively, in Church," "Oyster Bay," "Question," "Revival," "Stirhouse," "The Gift," "The Numbness," "The War," "True Faith," "Water Musik," "Worry Fills the Brim of My Hat";

Brilliant Corners: "American";

The Chattahoochee Review: "Surely the Wind";

The Colorado Review: "Down by the Old Mill Stream," "Elegy," "In Virginia," "Orphans," "Self-Portrait" (an earlier version of this poem appeared as "Memoir");

Cortland Review: "In Brooklyn";

Green River Review: "Because We've Failed So Often," "In My Little Paradise";

Kenyon Review: "Lament";

Massachusetts Review: "Ex-Wives";

Northwest Review: "America II," "The Sound and the Fury (1991)";

The Paris Review: "Heavens";

Prairie Schooner: "Apologia," "For Beauty" (an earlier version of this poem appeared as "Even the Rhapsody in Blue"), "In a Southern Climate" (originally titled "In the Current Climate").

"American" also appeared in *The Best American Poetry 2008*, edited by Charles Wright.

The poems in *Prairie Schooner* received the Glenna Luchei Prairie Schooner Award in 2007.

"Lament" was awarded the Lyric Poetry Prize by the Poetry Society of America.

I read a number of these poems aloud for the e-magazine *At the Fishhouse* (fishhousepoems.org).

Special thanks to Gerald Stern, Charles Simic, and Jane Mead for their encouragement and invaluable comments on poems in the manuscript.

About the Author

Ira Sadoff was born in Brooklyn, New York, on March 7, 1945. He earned a B.A. in industrial and labor relations from Cornell University and an M.F.A. from the University of Oregon. He is the author of seven earlier collections of poetry, a novel, *Uncoupling*, *The Ira Sadoff Reader*, and a book of criticism, *History Matters: Contemporary Poetry on the Margins of American Culture*. He is the recipient of fellowships from the National Endowment for the Arts and the John Simon Guggenheim Memorial Foundation. In 1973, he was a fellow at the Squaw Valley Community of Writers, and in 1974, he was the Alan Collins Fellow in Poetry and Prose at the Bread Loaf Writers' Conference. His poetry has been widely anthologized, including in *Harper American Literature*, *Great American Prose Poems*, and *The Best American Poetry* series in 2002 and 2008.

Sadoff has served as poetry editor of *The Antioch Review*, and was co-founder of *The Seneca Review*. He has taught at the Iowa Writers' Workshop, and in the M.F.A. programs of the University of Virginia and Warren Wilson College. He currently teaches in the M.F.A. program at Drew University, and serves as the Arthur Jeremiah Roberts Professor of English at Colby College, in Maine.

BOA Editions, Ltd.
American Poets Continuum Series

84

Colophon

True Faith, poems by Ira Sadoff, is set in Sabon, a digital version of the typeface designed by Jan Tschichold (1902–1974) and loosely based on the work of Claude Garamond and his pupil Jacques Sabon.

The publication of this book is made possible, in part, by the special support of the following individuals:

Anonymous

Anne Germanacos

Suzanne Gouvernet

Robin, Hollon & Casey Hursh,
in memory of Peter Hursh

X. J. & Dorothy M. Kennedy

Katherine Lederer

Boo Poulin

Deborah Ronnen & Sherm Levey

Steven O. Russell & Phyllis Rifkin Russell

Sue Stewart,
in memory of Steven L. Raymond

Ellen & David Wallack

Michael Waters & Mihaela Moscaliuc

Glenn & Helen William